PEARLS

Text and Photographs
Fred Ward

Editing
Charlotte Ward

Gifts from the sea. Many pearl fanciers believe today's cultured South Sea pearls represent the finest quality available. These near perfect examples, from Australia's northwest coast, illustrate what buyers seek: spheres with good color, high lustre, and sizes to 20mm. The smaller keshi *pearls, all-nacre naturals from 4.5mm to 7.5mm, usually result when epithelial cells accidentally enter oysters during nucleation.*

GUIDE TO
CULTURED PEARL
QUALITY

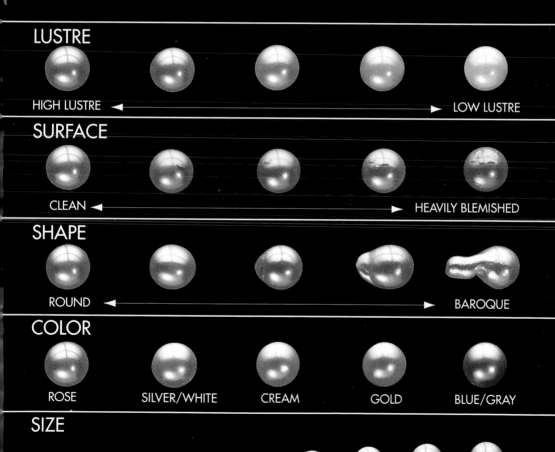

LUSTRE

HIGH LUSTRE ◄————————————————► LOW LUSTRE

SURFACE

CLEAN ◄————————————————► HEAVILY BLEMISHED

SHAPE

ROUND ◄————————————————► BAROQUE

COLOR

ROSE   SILVER/WHITE   CREAM   GOLD   BLUE/GRAY

SIZE

3mm   4mm   5mm   6mm   7mm   8mm   9mm   10mm

AUTHORIZED BY THE CULTURED PEARL ASSOCIATIONS OF AMERICA AND JAPAN

About Fred Ward and his Gem Book Series

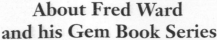

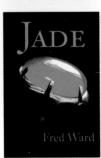

Glamour, intrigue, romance, the quest for treasure... those are all vital aspects of humankind's eternal search and love for gemstones. As long as people have roamed the world, they have placed extraordinary value on our incredible gifts from the land and sea.

Pearls is one of seven in a series of gem books written and photographed by Fred Ward. Each book, *Opals, Rubies & Sapphires, Emeralds, Diamonds, Pearls, Jade*, and *Gem Care*, is part of a 19-year global search into the history, geology, lore, and sources of these priceless treasures. He personally has visited the sites and artifacts displayed here to provide the most authentic and timely information available in the field. Fred Ward's original articles on these topics first appeared in *National Geographic* Magazine. In addition to being a journalist, Mr. Ward is a Graduate Gemologist (GIA), the highest academic achievement in the gem trade.

Mr. Ward, a respected authority on gems and gemology, is in great demand as a speaker to professional and private groups. After years viewing the gem trade around the world, he formed Blue Planet Gems, Inc. with designer Carol Tutera to make his vast experience available to others. Blue Planet Gems, Inc. specializes in fine custom-designed jewelry and private gem searches.

For those interested in printing mechanics, this book is part of the on-going computer revolution of desktop publishing. It was designed with PageMaker 6.5 layouts on a Power Computing 225. *Pearls* was printed by H & D Graphics.

HISTORY
AND LORE

Gifts from the sea and nature's most perfect and oft-repeated shape— pearls are both of these and more. Almost surely the world's first gem, pearls emerge from their watery homes without the need for cutting, faceting, or polishing. And, unlike some of their rare crystalline gem cousins with only a source or two, pearls are created by mollusks indigenous to almost every part of the world, living in lakes, rivers, and streams, in great oceans, as well as bays, inlets, lagoons, and atolls.

Long known as the *Queen of Gems*, pearls possess a history and allure far beyond what today's wearer may recognize. Throughout much of recorded history, a natural pearl necklace comprised of matched spheres was a treasure of almost incomparable value, in fact the most expensive jewelry in the world. Now we see pearls almost as accessories, relatively inexpensive decorations to accompany more costly gemstones. Before the creation of cultured pearls in the early 1900s, natural pearls were so rare and expensive that they were reserved almost exclusively for the noble and very rich. A jewelry item that today's working women take for granted, a 16-inch strand of perhaps 50 pearls, often costs between $500 and $3000. At the height of the Roman Empire, when pearl fever reached its peak, the historian Suetonius wrote that the Roman general Vitellius financed an entire military campaign by selling just one of his mother's pearl earrings.

No one will ever know who were the earliest people to collect and wear pearls. I suspect that the first pearls used as gems came from freshwater mussels. Without boats or equipment, primitive food gatherers must have found those mollusks much easier to obtain than oysters. Probably the first pearl fanciers sought mussels only after seeing animals enjoying the tasty meat. Since pearls themselves are indigestible unless crushed, people must have kept them for their beauty. Although few facts are available, surely early coastal societies also collected saltwater pearls.

A veil of more than 700 natural pearls adorns a 16th-century Russian Madonna and Child icon. Before the development of culturing in this century, all pearls were naturals, hence rare and valuable.

Treasury of the Munich Residenz

Most likely pearls were the first gems because they arrived from the sea ready to wear, needing no polishing or faceting. Although some were found in the Indian Ocean, the Red Sea, the Pacific, and the Caribbean, most of the world's saltwater natural pearls originated in the Persian Gulf (above). Stylish enough to enjoy today, this gold Egyptian earring (left) of Greco-Roman design is 2000 years old. Three natural pearls and rock crystals survive. A fourth pearl originally occupied the top opening.

National Museum, Cairo

George Frederick Kunz, whom I like to call America's first gemologist, in his 1908 masterpiece, *The Book of the Pearl*, states his belief that an ancient fish-eating tribe, perhaps along the coast of India, initially appreciated the shape and lustre of saltwater pearls, which they discovered while opening oysters for food. No matter the origin, a reverence for pearls spread throughout the world over the ensuing millennia. As reported in the oldest surviving religious and secular texts, pearls became almost universal symbols of beauty and value.

India's sacred books and epic tales abound with pearl references. One enduring myth names the gift from each element worthy of the deity: the air offered a rainbow, fire a meteor, earth a ruby, and the sea a pearl. One legend has the Hindu god Krishna discovering pearls when he plucks the first one from the sea and presents it to his daughter Pandaïa on her wedding day.

China's long recorded history provides ample evidence of the importance of pearls. In the Shu King, a 23rd-century B.C. book, the scribe sniffs that as tribute, a lesser king sent "strings of pearls not quite round."

Persia's glorious association with gems and jewelry also stretches for thousands of years (see pages 6-7). What Kunz describes as a magnificent

Unlimited time, resources, and access to natural pearls coalesced in India to create a royal market for fanciful confections like this 17th-18th-century seed pearl necklace: eighteen pearl balls each decorated with a ruby or an emerald, all held together by gold thread. Pearl slides complete the effect.

pearl necklace owned by a 4th-century B.C. princess now resides in the Louvre. In the nearby kingdom of Babylon, evidence of pearls and mother-of-pearl is even older. Mother-of-pearl inlays and decorations uncovered from Bismaya's ruins date from 4500 B.C. Across the Red Sea, in Egypt, decorative mother-of-pearl was used at least as far back as 4200 B.C., but the use of pearls themselves seems to have been later, perhaps related to the Persian conquest in the 5th century B.C. A few centuries later, as Rome set out to conquer the world and found itself in direct conflict with Egypt, pearls were the most valuable of all commodities. The story circulated in Rome that one reason Julius Caesar invaded Britain was in "hope of getting pearls." On another front, Roman cohorts arriving on the Nile in the 1st century B.C. found the Egyptian court enjoying pearls in abundance, whose value was almost beyond our comprehension.

Pearls played the pivotal role at the most celebrated banquet in literature. To convince Rome that Egypt possessed a heritage and wealth that put it above conquest, Cleopatra wagered Marc Antony she could give the most expensive dinner in history. The Roman reclined as the queen sat with an empty plate and a goblet of wine (or vinegar). She crushed one large pearl of a pair of earrings, dissolved it in the liquid, then drank it down. Astonished, Antony declined his dinner—the matching pearl—and admitted she had won. Pliny, the world's first gemologist, writes in his famous *Natural History* that the two pearls were worth an estimated 60 million sesterces, or 1,875,000 ounces of fine silver ($9,375,000, with silver at $5/ounce).

Perhaps the world's great religious texts state the poetry of pearls best; they repeatedly elevate them to the most exalted position. Christ speaks in Matthew saying, "The kingdom of heaven is like unto a merchant man, seeking goodly pearls: who, when he had found one pearl of great price, went and sold all that he had, and bought it." Also in Matthew,

Opulence almost beyond belief greets visitors to the Crown Jewels of Iran, sequestered in a bank vault in Tehran. A treasure chest of natural pearls from the Persian Gulf provided the monarchs a decorative inventory for regal paraphernalia.

In the Middle East, India, Persia, and Turkey, special reverence surrounds natural pearls, viewed as exquisite gifts from God. Until they were rivaled by the great 19th-century diamond discoveries, pearls were the most valuable of all gems.

Illustrating the regal appreciation of pearls are the personal adornments of Mary Queen of Scots, unfortunately beheaded in 1587. Her intricate gold rosary (below) incorporates natural saltwater pearls.

Her beautiful choker (right) is made of matched freshwater blister pearls from her beloved Scotland.

Arundel Castle, England (2)

Christ warns, "Neither cast ye your pearls before swine, lest they trample them under their feet, and turn again and rend you."

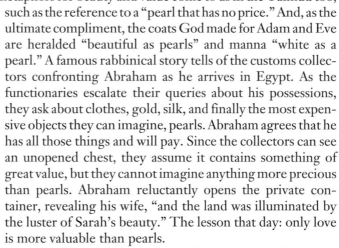

Pearl metaphors for beauty and value come to us in the Talmud too, such as the reference to a "pearl that has no price." And, as the ultimate compliment, the coats God made for Adam and Eve are heralded "beautiful as pearls" and manna "white as a pearl." A famous rabbinical story tells of the customs collectors confronting Abraham as he arrives in Egypt. As the functionaries escalate their queries about his possessions, they ask about clothes, gold, silk, and finally the most expensive objects they can imagine, pearls. Abraham agrees that he has all those things and will pay. Since the collectors can see an unopened chest, they assume it contains something of great value, but they cannot imagine anything more precious than pearls. Abraham reluctantly opens the private container, revealing his wife, "and the land was illuminated by the luster of Sarah's beauty." The lesson that day: only love is more valuable than pearls.

The Arabs have shown the greatest love for pearls. They have a history of the gems as old as India's. Today many Arabs will not buy cultured pearls, believing only natural pearls to be genuine. The depth of their affection for pearls is enshrined in the Koran, especially within its description of Paradise, which says, "The stones are pearls and jacinths; the fruits of the trees are pearls and emeralds; and each

A large natural baroque pearl forms the body of this late 16th-century European pendant. Enameled goldwork becomes wings for the hefty bird and support for a pair of almost round natural pearls. The eagle stands on a stylized gold branch intertwined with a blue and white enameled serpent. The base includes a large bezel-set cabochon ruby and a third round natural pearl suspended from its center.

Victoria and Albert Museum, London

person admitted to the delights of the celestial kingdom is provided with a tent of pearls, jacinths, and emeralds; is crowned with pearls of incomparable lustre, and is attended by beautiful maidens resembling hidden pearls."

R ome's pearl craze reached its zenith during the 1st century B.C. Never before had pearls been so expensive yet so abundant. Military conquests brought opulence, and with it, excess. Roman women upholstered couches with pearls and sewed so many into their gowns that they actually walked on their pearl-encrusted hems. Caligula, having made his horse a consul, decorated it with a pearl necklace. Nero provided his actors with scepters and masks laden with the ocean gems. Whereas few dared to complain about emperors' extravagances, a peevish Seneca notes how many pearls hang from the ears of patrician women: "The lobes of our ladies have attained a special capacity for supporting a great number."

Considering how precious pearls were and how many of them must have been required through the centuries to satisfy the cravings of the ostentatious Romans and others, it might appear paradoxical that so few artifacts remain. Pearls are not as durable as gold, bronze, crystal gems, or even glass. In fact, they are comparatively delicate gems, produced by living creatures. Although for daily care, pearls do best in relatively consistent medium humidity, centuries-long preservation as artifacts depends mainly upon burial in dry conditions. Some pearls unearthed in North Africa's deserts (see pages 4 and 10) are remarkably well preserved. Most are more like those uncovered in Emperor Honorius' tomb, sealed in Rome for 12

Elizabeth Taylor owns **La Peregrina** *(The Wanderer) one of the few named pearls. Found off Panama in the 1500s, it was purchased by Richard Burton in 1969 for $37,000. Wealthy Egyptians, including Cleopatra, whom Ms. Taylor played in her famous role, prized natural pearls above crystal gemstones.*

Egypt traded Arab dealers for Red Sea, Persian Gulf, and Indian pearls. In the Greco-Roman period (300 B.C.-300 A.D.) Egyptian ladies wore elaborate gold and pearl earrings (above).

centuries. The ruler's other ornaments were relatively intact, but as Kunz observes, the pearls were "as lusterless and dead as a wreath of last year's flowers." A sad loss.

During the long history of pearls, the principal oyster beds lay in the Persian Gulf, along the coasts of India and Ceylon (now Sri Lanka), and in the Red Sea. Chinese pearls came mainly from freshwater rivers and ponds, whereas Japanese pearls were found near the coast in salt water. Nearly all the pearls in commerce originated from those few sources. Over the next millennium only three substantive events altered what appeared to be a very stable pattern. Considering the minimal state of pearling in the United States today, it is impressive that two of the three developments occurred in the New World.

As Europe raced to capitalize on what Columbus had stumbled upon, the major powers of the day concentrated on spheres of influence. Except for Florida, Mexico, Texas, and California, Spain focused its efforts in Central and South America and the Caribbean. The English colonizers along North America's Atlantic coast and French explorers to the north and west, all found native Americans wearing pearls. The British and French discovered freshwater pearls in the Ohio, Mississippi, and Tennessee River basins. Along both the Atlantic and Pacific coasts of Central America, the Spanish forced slaves to dive for pearls. So many gems were exported to Europe that the New World quickly gained the appellation "Land of Pearls."

What is now the United States became famous for two products. Its best freshwater pearls fueled a ready market overseas, purchased by people

Victoria and Albert Museum, London (3)

By the early 19th century, mastery of the medium and a steady supply of natural pearls from the Persian Gulf and Indian Ocean allowed European artisans the freedom to express their pearl fantasies in complicated new shapes, such as grape vines and bows. A new source of freshwater pearls, the recently independent United States, provided large rounds, as seen throughout the grapevine necklace (ca. 1835).

who, unlike the then less sophisticated frontier Americans, knew the rarity and value of large round lustrous pearls. Many of the best examples made their way into Europe's royal gem collections, where they can still be seen on display, usually misidentified as saltwater pearls from the Orient.

The vast freshwater mussel beds, which produced fabulous pearls, also became a major source for a different product. America exported mother-of-pearl buttons all over the world. Iowa became the center of the trade, shipping billions of iridescent fasteners until World War II, when newly invented plastic virtually drove quality buttons out of the market.

While North America set a new standard for large freshwater pearls, white saltwater pearls from the coasts of Panama and Venezuela competed with pearls from Bahrain, and black saltwater pearls from the Bay of California (in what is now Mexico) provided an alternative to Tahitian blacks. More pearls arrived in Spain than the country's aristocratic market could absorb. As with the emeralds it was mining in Colombia, Spain found ready buyers for its new pearls across Europe and in India.

Those pearl supplies continued into the 1800s, until overfishing in Central American waters and in North American streams depleted the beds. Pollution also took its toll as the United Stated industrialized. Then, toward the end of the last century, the single event that forever reshaped the pearl trade slowly unfolded in the isolated island nation of Japan.

Expansion into the pearl trade began when Japan's usually insular people pioneered a mother-of-pearl business along the north coast of Australia during the last half of the 19th century. By the early 1900s, Broome, a tiny coastal outpost that looks like the quintessential Aussie outback, sold

more than three quarters of the world's mother-of-pearl. What Australian traders and Japanese discovered was that huge silver-lipped and golden-lipped South Sea oysters produce prodigious amounts of gorgeous mother-of-pearl. Diving for shells was to be a venture with great personal risks for entrepreneurs and divers alike. Japan's offshore expansion into mother-of-pearl collection paved the way for its later moves into cultured pearling. Pearl culturing, a monumental development in the Japanese home islands, created a new relationship between Japan, Australia, and other Pacific countries that changed the pearl business forever.

Kokichi Mikimoto, the son of a noodle maker, had a dream and a hard-working wife, Ume. Together they set about to do what no one else had done—entice oysters to produce round pearls on demand. Mikimoto may not have known that the Chinese had successfully produced pearl Buddhas inside mussels since the 1200s. Today we would call them freshwater *mabés*. It is clear that he did not know that government biologist Tokichi Nishikawa and carpenter Tatsuhei Mise had each independently discovered the secret of pearl culturing—inserting a piece of oyster epithelial membrane (the lip of mantle tissue) with a nucleus of shell or metal into an oyster's body or mantle causes the tissue to form a pearl sack. That sack then secretes nacre to coat the nucleus, thus creating a cultured pearl.

    Mise received a 1907 patent for his grafting needle. When Nishikawa applied for a patent for nucleating, he realized that he and Mise had discovered the same procedure. In a compromise, the pair signed an agreement uniting their common discovery as the Mise-Nishikawa method, which

In the late 1800s beautiful, huge shells lured thousands of Japanese divers to seek mother-of-pearl in Australia, where many died (far left). But their pioneer work opened Japan's eyes to business prospects in the South Pacific. At home, Kokichi Mikimoto mastered pearl culturing, transforming the trade by promoting his new products. At expositions he displayed crowns, the Liberty Bell, and temples made of cultured pearls.

remains the heart of pearl culturing. Mikimoto had received an 1896 patent for producing hemispherical pearls, or mabés, and a 1908 patent for culturing in mantle tissue. But he could not use the Mise-Nishikawa method without invalidating his own patents. So he altered his patent application to cover a technique to make *round* pearls in mantle tissue, which was granted in 1916. With that technicality, Mikimoto began an unprecedented expansion, buying rights to the Mise-Nishikawa method and eclipsing those originators of cultured pearls, leaving their names only for history books.

Largely by trial and error over a number of years, Mikimoto did contribute one crucial discovery. Whereas Nishikawa nucleated with silver and gold beads, Mikimoto experimented with everything from glass to lead to clay to wood. He found he had the highest success rates when he inserted round nuclei cut from U.S. mussel shells. Although U.S. mussel shells were the basis for virtually all cultured saltwater pearls for 90 years, several countries are now experimenting with other nuclei material.

Even though third with his patents and his secrets, Mikimoto revolutionized pearling. Ever the flamboyant showman and promoter, he badgered jewelers and governments to accept his cultured products as pearls. His workers created massive pearl structures, which he displayed at every major international exposition. By mastering the techniques, Mikimoto, then hundreds of other Japanese firms, made pearls available to virtually everyone in the world. What was once rare and costly became affordable. In the process, the market for natural pearls evaporated. Today naturals are sought only by collectors, members of some religious sects, a few Europeans, and many Arabs. Cultured pearls are now the market.

NATURAL
PEARLS

Today's snorkeling and sports diving are comfortable recreational experiences. Natural pearl diving never was. A diver in the Persian Gulf wore a loincloth and nothing else except leather finger protectors. He had no mask and no breathing apparatus. After a few deep breaths on the surface, he stepped into a hoop in a rope tied to a 30-to-50-pound rock. Once a worker released his rope, the diver, rock, and a basket to hold oysters plunged to the bottom, 30 to 60 feet below. From here it was a race against time. Holding his breath, he scrambled around in the sand and rocks. With saltwater burning his eyes and blurring his vision, he felt for oysters, placing them into the basket as he minded the time. Most divers stayed down no more than a minute. Every now and then a man might stay two.

A sharp tug on the rope set the attendant on the boat to pulling, bringing up diver, rock, and basket. The diver's ears must have popped and his sinuses ached. He rose with the haunting fear of shark attack. After resting 5 to 10 minutes topside, he cycled through another of 40 or more daily dives. It was a tough, dangerous, poor-paying business. A good bed might have yielded a dozen oysters each dive, but often he came up empty handed. A diver's pay was a negotiated percentage from the sale of pearls he found. On the surface workers opened shells. Sometimes they poked through hundreds to thousands of oysters to harvest a single quality pearl.

For almost the entire history of pearling, that simple harvesting process did not change. The most productive oyster beds were well known and regularly worked for centuries. Frederick Kunz wryly characterizes Bahrain as late as 1906: "The fishery in this region owes absolutely nothing to modern civilization..." What was true of harvesting was also true of the treatment of the day, bleaching. When the boats docked, the darker natural pearls were placed on rugs on the beaches to sun-bleach. Some were "peeled" to remove blemishes. After sorting, pearls were ready for dealers.

Pearl exports closely followed the global politics of the day. More than

A 16th-century flight of fancy transforms a magnificent natural baroque pearl into a warrior merman's torso. The "Canning Jewel" was crafted in Italy of enamel, pearls, and gemstones and presented by a Medici prince to the Mogul emperor of India, who added its dangling ruby floret.

Victoria and Albert Museum, London

History shows little change in the natural pearl trade for more than 2000 years before World War II. Arab fleets with 35,000 or more divers, often financed by Indian traders, worked the Persian Gulf's oyster beds, particularly around Bahrain.

As demand for pearls grew in the 18th and 19th centuries, European buyers came directly to the source (below). Fifty or more Arab divers worked on each of hundreds of pearl boats in the late 1880s (right). Divers held their breath for one to two minutes, free-diving to 60 feet, and grappled by hand for a few shells. Ceylon shells, prized for superior color, were sorted in open sheds before auctions (left).

Les barques — dont certaines portent 50 pêcheurs — rassemblées pour le travail sur les bancs d'huîtres perlières.
Une planche, fixée contre le bord, permet aux plongeurs de se reposer après qu'ils sont remontés et avant de se replonger à nouveau dans les eaux de la mer.

Over several centuries Persian rulers assembled one of the world's greatest gem collections, the Crown Jewels of Iran, then used it to back the national treasury. When the last shah was crowned in 1967, he incorporated natural pearls and gemstones from the collection into a new Crown of State (above), which features a 60-carat centerstone and 3,380 other diamonds. For his queen, Farah, he made a crown (opposite, right) with 105 pearls, 36 emeralds, 34 rubies, and 1469 diamonds. The collection includes many natural pearl and bejeweled turban decorations (opposite, left).

18

2000 years ago, pearls were marketed in Baghdad or Bombay and destined for Greece, Egypt, or Rome. For the next 1000 years or so, Indian, Persian, Turkish, and Middle Eastern rulers bought. With the rise of European royalty from the Renaissance forward, the market shifted again. European brokers gathered their supplies by appearing on shore to haggle directly with the pearlers.

Until this century, all the pearls that ever grew inside oysters and mussels over eons and all the pearls treasured by people for the past few thousand years had been natural saltwater and freshwater pearls. Freshwater naturals are not as well known as their saltwater counterparts, although comparable pearls from both sources are similarly priced. In reality, most of the very best freshwater naturals were usually sold as saltwater pearls. While doing the original research for my *National Geographic* pearl article and for this book, I found great U.S. natural freshwater pearls in museums all over the world displayed as saltwater pearls. Except in Germany, where it is known that Bavarian rivers produced fine pearls, most curators are unaware where their natural pearls originated.

What exactly are natural pearls? Why were they so rare and valuable that Cartier acquired its New York headquarters in the 1920s by trading a matron her town house for two strands of natural saltwater pearls, priced then at more than a million dollars?

Like clams and other mollusks, oysters and mussels build their own shell homes and keep them clean and tidy. The creatures build by constantly secreting layers of hexagonal aragonite crystals of calcium carbonate, which we call mother-of-pearl if it coats the inside of a shell and nacre if it covers a pearl. Within their hard exterior shells, oysters and mussels are surprisingly delicate, lacking skeleton, fur, or hardy covering. They cannot tolerate

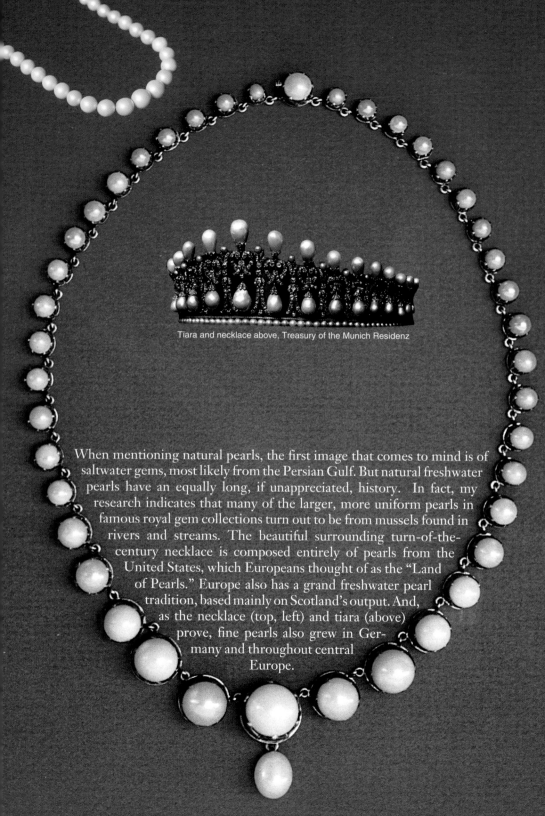

Tiara and necklace above, Treasury of the Munich Residenz

When mentioning natural pearls, the first image that comes to mind is of saltwater gems, most likely from the Persian Gulf. But natural freshwater pearls have an equally long, if unappreciated, history. In fact, my research indicates that many of the larger, more uniform pearls in famous royal gem collections turn out to be from mussels found in rivers and streams. The beautiful surrounding turn-of-the-century necklace is composed entirely of pearls from the United States, which Europeans thought of as the "Land of Pearls." Europe also has a grand freshwater pearl tradition, based mainly on Scotland's output. And, as the necklace (top, left) and tiara (above) prove, fine pearls also grew in Germany and throughout central Europe.

Necklace, private U.S. collection

anything sharp inside their shells, so they rely on a defense mechanism. Because the creatures feed by inhaling and exhaling water, debris constantly flows in and out. Most of the time the animals easily flush away irritants. But occasionally a piece of shell, coral, or bone hooks into the flesh. Unable to excrete the intruder, the oyster or mussel does the next best thing. It coats the abrasive irritant with nacre, making the foreign particle smooth and tolerable. A natural pearl is born.

Sometimes natural pearl making begins with an alien creature, a parasite. If a worm or snail attaches itself to an oyster's flesh, the host may coat the parasite with nacre too. Sometimes a drilling mollusk bores through a valve, and the oyster covers the hole, producing a "blister pearl" on the inside surface of its shell. Those are most often like mabés, and not real pearls. Sand, which usually gets credit for precipitating natural pearl growth, is never involved—oysters easily expel sand.

Enormous quality differences separate natural and cultured saltwater pearls. Natural pearls are by definition all pearl. There are no implanted nuclei, as you will see inside cultured pearls in the following chapter. All-nacre pearls, like some of the Egyptian examples in the first chapter, can last for centuries. Nacre depth also produces another benefit, a full-bodied lustre and beauty unequaled by a thin nacre coating. When you look into a rich, iridescent natural pearl, the light deeply penetrates the interior of the pearl, producing a sense of solidity as well as a luminous color impossible to replicate by culturing with a shell nucleus.

With virtually no natural-pearl collecting now anywhere in the world, you would think that demand from the *cognoscenti* would be enormous. Instead, except for a small market for astrological pundits, few U.S. buyers will pay premium for naturals. However, the market is considerably different overseas, where quality remains a criterion. Europeans value naturals, and Arabs will almost never buy anything else. Their relatively small demand is met mainly by reselling old strands. In an environment-conscious world, no government is likely to allow the devastation associated with oyster collection on a scale needed to produce natural pearl necklaces.

How often do oysters and mussels produce natural pearls? Rarely, as it turns out. There is some variation from country to country, but Trish Grey, a partner in an Australian pearl farm, told me in Broome, "Once we brought up a hundred tons of shells for mother-of-pearl without finding a single pearl worth $100." Frederick Kunz estimated it would take at least 100,000 oysters from Bahrain to get enough pearls for one necklace. And John Latendresse in Tennessee says he gets about 1½ ounces of pearl from a ton of shell, of which only 15 percent is usable for jewelry. But finding natural pearls is just the first step. With no shell sphere as a nucleus, naturals are almost never round or uniform in size. The rarity of quality natural pearls, particularly when matched by size, shape, and color, was a major reason for the extraordinary prices they commanded in Rome, as well as during the pearl craze in Europe and the United States in the 1920s.

In the Roaring 1920s Mikimoto reached full production. America's new rich were just becoming a market force when the "pearl crash" of 1930

K.C. Bell collection

Any shellfish can produce pearls, either full pearls inside the creatures' bodies or blister pearls on shell surfaces. American Indians used decorative iridescent abalone shells for thousands of years. Natural abalone pearls (above) fetch fancy prices, up to $100,000 for a necklace like this. Because they form inside the animal's body, baroque shapes, called "dog's teeth" and "horns," are pearls too.

Native Americans treasured pearls perhaps as long as 10,000 years ago. A freshwater pearl necklace from the Hopewell Indian mounds in Ohio (opposite, left) was worn as early as 1000 B.C. American pearls have no equal, as seen in the fabulous 17.2mm-pink freshwater natural from Arkansas (opposite, right).

With only 4 gems per 50,000 shells, conch pearls are rare enough to entice collectors to pay several hundred to several thousand dollars apiece. When conch shells were common in the Florida Keys, pearls were readily available. Now illegal to collect in the United States, conch, whose shells are the raw material of cameos, come mainly from the Bahamas and from Caribbean islands further south. In addition to their unique orange color, fine-quality conch pearl examples exhibit an easily identifiable "flame" pattern.

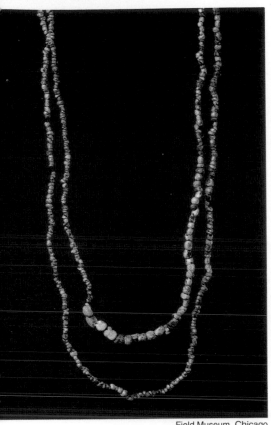

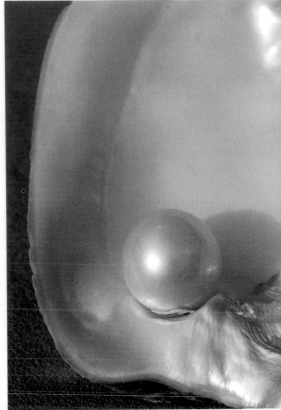

collapsed natural pearl prices. People saw their investments plummet as Mikimoto's new cultured pearls gained increasing acceptance. A casual observer could see little difference between a half-million-dollar strand of naturals and a strand of Japanese imports, which Mikimoto sold until the 1940s for less than $100. Global cultured pearl promotion and global war delivered a one-two punch from which natural pearl sales never recovered.

World War II disrupted the worldwide pearl trade, both natural and cultured. While natural pearlers could not work, Mikimoto kept his farms open, stockpiling for after the war. Although war activities seriously damaged the great Persian Gulf and Indian Ocean oyster beds, other influences sealed their demise. Demand for naturals ended with the popularity of cultured pearls. The simultaneous discovery and wild exploration for oil in the Gulf area brought devastating pollution to oysters. The pearl work force gravitated to jobs related to war, petroleum, and industrialization in the region, all fatal to natural pearling.

After the war, Japan directed enormous resources to culturing. Even though the practice was then less than fifty years old, the Japanese actually called the new business their "national heritage." Postwar baby-boomers readily accepted cultured products as pearls so that cultured pearls became the pearl market. New York gem dealer Maurice Shire says, "In the 1920s there were 300 U.S. natural pearl dealers. By the 1950s we were down to 6, and now none. The natural pearl business is dead."

CULTURED
SALTWATER
PEARLS

Once Mikimoto expanded until he had 12 million oysters in the water producing 75 percent of the world's pearls, he could not keep other Japanese from learning how to culture pearls. But he and they did elevate his discoveries to the status of national treasures. They refused to publish or to share the technology. As consumers wanted pearls larger than Japanese *akoya* oysters (*Pinctada imbricata*) could produce, Japanese farmers sought larger South Seas oysters, expanding pearling to Thursday Island first, then to Burma. To participate in the pearl trade, other countries had to allow Japanese technicians to nucleate oysters and harvest pearls, and the pearls had to return to Japan for marketing. Beginning in the 1960s, cultured pearl operations spread across the warm Pacific, from Burma to Australia, the Philippines, Indonesia, Tahiti, Thailand, the Cook Islands, and to an increasing number of smaller islands.

Then, through laws, associations, a cartel, and private agreements, Japan sought to extend its monopoly of the world's cultured pearl trade by saying it would produce all pearls up to 10mm within Japan and that only pearls larger than 10mm could be grown elsewhere if they were returned to Japan for marketing. Amazingly, for three decades other countries followed that directive, until events outpaced Japan's conservative ability to react. First, some independent Australians and their government rebelled at Japan's control. Then the sleeping Chinese giant awakened, asserting its sovereignty and earning hard currency by pearling. In the 1990s, Japan has continually had to defend its territory in the trade.

These fine examples of Japanese akoya pearls exhibit the high lustre and dyed pink color preferred by the U.S. market. Mikimoto maintains its uniform quality standard by combining pearls it grows with pearls it buys. Pearls are then sorted for size, shape, lustre, and color.

*Modern cultured pearling
began a few miles from Japan's
Ago Bay, pictured above filled
with pearl rafts. Oysters
maturing until they are large
enough for nucleation, as well
as nucleated oysters producing
pearls, hang below rows of
bamboo rafts (right).*

*Japanese pearl farms no longer
use wild oysters. They hatch
oysters from eggs in large glass
tanks (opposite, left). The tiny
white vulnerable hatchlings, or
spat, must have solid support.
They attach instantly to plastic
strips (opposite, top right).*

*Farm spat, which never tumble
in the ocean, feed entirely on a
prepared diet (opposite, bottom
right). Consequently, they
will never be as strong
as wild akoya.*

26

C ulturing pearls at Ago Bay has changed since Mr. Mikimoto opened his farms in the early 1900s. He had moved from the nearby port town of Toba to find clean water and a rural environment. But now that the land around the bay has been developed, the water is no longer clean enough for pearls. More and more, pearl farmers are looking first to Japan's southern island, Kyushu, then to other Pacific sites. With China expanding rapidly into saltwater culturing, the Japanese find themselves increasingly noncompetitive as pearl farmers, evolving by necessity into marketers of China's pearls. Higher salaries, weaker oysters, and more polluted waters in Japan make competition with China very difficult. During the disastrous 1996 harvest, half of Japan's pearl oysters died, an estimated 148 million.

Were he to return, Mikimoto would first notice that pearl farms no longer employ bare-breasted Ama divers to find young healthy akoya in the ocean. Now baby oysters hatch in glass tanks inside onshore laboratories. Once the oysters grow large enough to live outside, workers transfer them to baskets under rafts in the bay. In the spring of their third year, when they are healthiest and most active, oysters are nucleated with a shell bead and mantle tissue. Pearls are harvested in the coldest months, when lustre is at its highest.

After exhaustive experiments, Mikimoto decided that about four years in the water was best for quality pearls. To cut costs and accelerate income, many Japanese pearl farmers over the past decade have systematically slashed the culturing time to $2\frac{1}{2}$ years, then to $1\frac{1}{2}$ years, and finally to less than 6 months. Today, the length of time between nucleation and harvest is at the heart of the greatest controversy surrounding cultured pearls—short culture times. Nacre thickness is barely more than a cosmetic coating. The burden has shifted to the consumer to find pearls with sufficient nacre

For eight decades Japan guarded pearl culturing as a "national secret." Now many countries know the procedure. Baskets of 3-year-old oysters arrive from the rafts (left). A worker cuts strips of live mantle tissue from a sacrificed oyster (above).

Nucleators wedge open the waiting oysters (opposite, top) and make a quick scalpel cut into the soft flesh. Based on the size and health of the oyster, they decide instantly what diameter and how many shell nuclei to press into the incision (opposite, right). A piece of live mantle tissue goes in with each nucleus before the oyster is allowed to close its shell.

thickness to last through even one lifetime of wear.

In Japan, workers usually nucleate onshore near the rafts that hold suspended oysters. Increasingly, other countries nucleate on boats or rafts to shorten the time oysters are out of the water and to reduce land-borne contaminants. Wherever Japanese technicians operate, they use the same procedures. They bring up the oysters and immediately squeeze them into baskets. After half an hour, when the pressure on the oysters is released, the oysters instinctively relax their muscles. Capitalizing on that reflex action, a woman quickly pushes in a plastic wedge to hold the shells, or valves, apart.

In this condition the oysters are delivered to nucleators (typically women inside Japan and men overseas), each sitting before a holding stand, a tray of various-sized shell beads (nuclei), and small pieces of mantle tissue from a just-sacrificed oyster. Placing a new oyster in a holder, the nucleator inserts a spring-loaded scissors device, called a dilator, beside the plastic wedge, forcing open the oyster's shell. Looking inside the narrow opening, the nucleator decides instantly about the oyster's position, size, and health, then quickly incises the flesh with a surgeon's scalpel. Inside the slit goes one or more shell nuclei, along with a piece of mantle tissue for each bead, and a drop of antiseptic to reduce infection. Then the nucleator removes the dilator, allowing the oyster to close its shell. Within minutes nucleated oysters are returned to baskets under nearby rafts, where about half either eject the nuclei or die.

Almost all Japanese and South Sea cultured pearls are nucleated with spheres cut from U.S. freshwater mussel shells from the Tennessee River/Mississippi River systems. Until recently, the majority of all those shells passed through John Latendresse's Canton, Tennessee, warehouse (left), usually filled with stuffed burlap bags destined for Japan. John sold the shell business to concentrate on his pearl culturing, but U.S. shells remain vital to the world pearl trade.

Inside a Cultured Pearl...

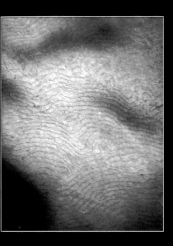

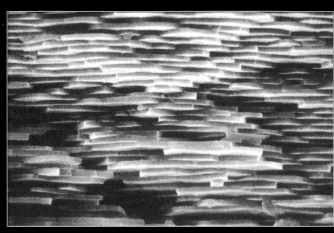

Fingerprint-like surface deposits characterize both natural and cultured pearls (above, left). Those features, easily seen under magnification, assist in separating pearls from glass, plastic, and fish-scale imitations. The slight texture is also what you feel if you touch a pearl to your front teeth.

Most of a saltwater cultured pearl is a shell sphere nucleus implanted as an irritant in a live oyster. The quality and durability of the resulting pearl is mainly determined by the nacre layers the oyster builds around that nucleus. All other quality concerns are secondary to nacre thickness, which determines how long a pearl will last.

The oyster coats a nucleus the same way it builds its shell home, by depositing repeated layers of nacre formed by secretions from the animal's mantle tissue (nacre layers in cross-section, above, right). Inserting a shell nucleus with a piece of mantle tissue is the heart of Japanese pearl culturing. Whereas a natural pearl results from the accidental introduction of an irritant into an oyster, which then coats it to reduce discomfort, the concept of a cultured pearl is to begin with a shell bead almost as big as the final pearl and induce the oyster to coat the shell nucleus.

In each sliced pearl below, notice the shell bead nucleus in the center of the pearl, surrounded by an outer layer of nacre. South Seas pearls usually have substantially more nacre than Japanese akoyas. A pearl with 0.40mm of nacre should last through a lifetime of normal wear. More nacre is obviously better and less is risky. Thin-coated pearls do not last. They crack around the drill holes and lack depth in their color, lustre, or both.

South Sea Pearl
Nacre = 2.05mm

Akoya Pearl
Nacre = 0.95mm

Akoya Pearl
Nacre = 0.40mm

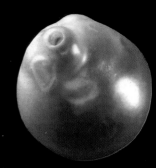

The industry processes cultured pearls considerably more than it likes to admit. The less processing (bleaching, dyeing, polishing), the better. But Japanese pearl producers insist matched pearls in a necklace would cost a fortune if the pearls were not made uniform after harvesting. Although the Japanese continue denying they process their products a decade after I first revealed the practices in my National Geographic article, the reality is that virtually all Japanese cultured pearls are first bleached, then dyed, and often polished. Pearls are bleached in a mild heated bath under bright fluorescent lights (above, left). That Japanese pearls are later dyed is easily seen by observing pearls in their true colors at the harvest. Dyeing is done to suit the market; Americans prefer pink. Look down the drill hole of a bright pink pearl to see the spongy dyed red conchiolin layer around the nucleus (above, right).

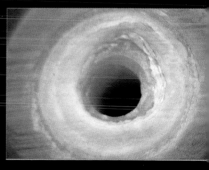

Nacre thickness is determined by studying either x-rays or cultured pearl drill holes (right). There is a distinct color and texture break where the nacre coating meets the shell-bead nucleus. In the examples below, the small pearl is adequately coated, but the 0.20mm nacre coating will not last. Too many such pearls are being sold to unsuspecting buyers. And the backlit pearl (lower right) has so little nacre that the shell striations show through clearly, indicating nacre that may flake off within months.

Small Akoya Pearl
Nacre – 0.40mm

Akoya Pearl
Nacre = 0.20mm

Akoya Pearl
Nacre = <0.1mm

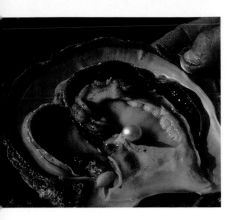

Australia produces the largest, most expensive cultured pearls in the world, which most insiders consider to be the finest. Off the country's northwestern coast, divers gather young wild oysters. Once oysters mature in baskets, they are nucleated at sea, often by Japanese technicians, and returned to the water to produce richly-coated yellow, gold, and white 10mm to 20mm pearls (above, left). With Japan's oyster problems, Australian farmers have begun cultivating pearls down to 7mm.

Japan forged close ties with Australia beginning at Kuri Bay in 1956 (above, right). The partnership worked almost unchanged for decades, with Australians providing licenses, boats, and workers while the Japanese supplied technicians, know-how, and global marketing of finished pearls. Each pearl farm was jointly owned by Japanese and Australian companies. Control is slowly changing as super-entrepreneurs, such as Nick Paspaley, whose farms produce half of Australia's pearl output, and George Kailis slowly maneuver the Japanese into the background. They and others now deal with buyers directly and establish prices. To break a former monopoly, by law pearl farmers must teach Australians the Japanese nucleating techniques.

Immobilized oysters must be rotated and cleaned to keep them healthy, which is usually done by raising the containment baskets to the surface. Instead, pearl farmer Bruce Farley braves powerful currents to flop his baskets (below), taking advantage of the nutrient-laden 30- to 40-foot tides off Broome to feed his nucleated oysters.

Roebuck Deep Pearls

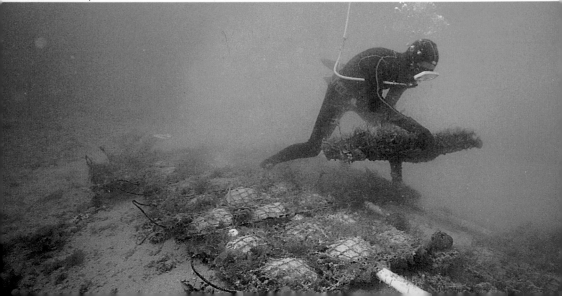

These exquisite golden South Sea pearls (above), owned by the government of Myanmar, may be the best matched set ever assembled. Burma was once famous for such pearls, but not any more.

Illustrating the usual color range of Australian South Sea pearls, (below, left) we see four marvelous examples. And an Australian baroque pearl was the inspiration for this circus seal, balancing a blue sapphire. And best of all, a perfect gold Australian South Sea pearl (below), approaching 20mm, is one of the largest ever grown.

Fred Ward

Paspaley Pearls Pty. Ltd. (2)

China has quietly increased its saltwater efforts so rapidly that it is now a major pearl producer. With thousands of miles of inlets and shoreline (above) and water temperatures from tropical to temperate, China poses increasing competition to Japanese and South Sea farmers with pearls up to 10mm. Already Chinese success with freshwater and saltwater pearls has driven Japan to limit its production of 4mm, 5mm, and 6mm pearls.

Using Japanese techniques and locally produced shell nuclei, nucleators at a government farm south of Canton (left) implant akoya oysters that will mature in nearby coves.

China looms as the driving force for change as cultured pearls pass their 100th birthday. Targeting freshwater pearls first, China completely overtook Japan a decade ago and virtually owns the global freshwater trade today. As China increases saltwater pearl culturing, Japanese pearl firms are attempting to tie up agreements to process and market their new material. If China increases production dramatically and continues to sell much of its output independently, prices will fall.

Quality remains the main issue. No one knows how such a huge, decentralized country can control quality when it has tens of thousands of individual farms producing pearls. The free market is at work as dealers from overseas, from Hong Kong, and from inside China comb the countryside carrying U.S. and Hong Kong dollars, setting prices on the spot. The government has basically lost control. Pearls cultured in China show up in U.S. and European stores usually tagged "Product of Japan" or "Made in Hong Kong." Unfortunately, as the Chinese learned culturing and

Experiments in the 1980s convinced China that its cleaner waters and inexpensive labor could help it dominate saltwater pearl production (left). With similar climate and oysters to Japan's, China realized it needed only Japan's technical information. For nearly two decades China's pearl culturers have been concentrating on improving skills and forming trade agreements with Japan in return for allowing Japanese firms to process and market Chinese pearls. Both Chinese freshwater and saltwater pearls routinely sell to U.S. dealers and consumers marked "Product of Japan."

processing techniques from the Japanese, they also picked up the bad Japanese practice of short culturing their new pearls, which they are selling mainly within China. Short-cultured pearls are not bargains at any price.

China's extensive coastline ranges from temperate to tropical. It already produces akoya pearls in traditional Japanese sizes and larger South Sea pearls at Hainan Island. With very few exceptions, before the late 1980s there were only two kinds of cultured saltwater pearls—those up to 10mm grown in Japan and those larger than 10mm produced in various other countries around the Pacific. Unquestionably the Japanese over 9 decades developed techniques and experience that put them ahead of other saltwater pearl farmers. But now China has replaced Japan to dominate in the smaller sizes. China soon may be the world's largest saltwater pearl producer just as it already is the largest producer of freshwater pearls. Only time will tell whether China can produce saltwater pearls equal to Japan's former quality. No one knows if China will market independent of Japan. Such a development could realign the pearl trade to provide more pearls at lower prices with a look different from naturals or bygone iridescent akoya. Now Japanese dealers buy Chinese pearls for 30 percent less than Japan's akoya, mark them up, and sell them labeled "Product of Japan."

Encouraged by China's rapid success in freshwater culturing, several other pearl-producing countries are moving toward independence from Japan. Australia, in particular, already does more than it used to of its own nucleating and marketing. Venezuela, Mexico, India, and Thailand, all with the water and technical skills, may soon be tempted. Australia has led the way with direct marketing and auctions, increasingly cutting out the Japanese and their profits as middlemen to the world's pearl dealers.

No matter the outcome for akoya, growers will continue to harvest the big ones, pearls above 10mm, from the blue lagoons of the South Seas.

For matchless caché in gems, black pearls from Polynesia (left) represent a level of sophistication reflected in their prices. Just as white-lipped oysters in Australia produce gorgeous South Sea white pearls, Tahiti's black-lipped oysters (below, right) yield unique iridescent black and gray pearls. After nucleation, oysters hang on lines (above) in dreamy aquamarine lagoons, building the dark nacre that distinguishes these pearls. Black pearl pioneer Jean-Claude Brouillet (below, left) sorts his harvest outdoors.

This necklace with ruby enhancer first sold in the 1980s for less than $200,000. A necklace of 27 large black pearls, auctioned in the mid-1990s in New York for almost $800,000, immediately sold in Japan at twice the auction price. Because Tahitian pearls come in so many shades of gray, black, and greenish black, matching pearls for necklaces is difficult and time consuming.

Due to heavy advertising, demand for black pearls recently rose 5 to 10 percent annually. That success caused black pearl farmers in the Cook Islands and other South Sea atolls to increase production, which precipitated a drop in wholesale prices of 25 to 40 percent.

Throughout the warm waters of the Pacific, black-lipped oysters (*Pinctada margaritifera*) produce a rich array of black, gray, and iridescent greenish black pearls that capture the imaginations of venturesome buyers. Long sought for their unique appeal, black pearls bring an aura of exclusivity to any piece of jewelry. In the days when all pearls were natural, black pearls were royal treasures, particularly coveted by England's Elizabeth I.

Employing Japanese techniques and technicians as the Australians did to make white pearls, farmers in French Polynesia grew the first large cultured blacks in 1969. They began near Tahiti and have since spread out over a thousand miles through the island chain. Supported and encouraged by the government's export promotion authority, *G.I.E. Perles de Tahiti*, black pearl advertising has paid off. Individual strands may have pearls from 8mm to 20mm, with 14mm-strands often selling for $20,000 to $50,000.

Even though their products and prices are somewhat comparable, Polynesians have lagged behind Australians in taking nucleation and marketing control from the Japanese. Far more important to Polynesia's future is the proliferation of black pearl operations across the Pacific. It seems that every island with black-lipped oysters wants to profit from black pearls.

Among the more interesting newcomers to black pearl farming are the Cook Islanders, who have begun culturing with the full assistance and cooperation of their government. Having bought the Japanese technician and marketing package, they are already producing black rounds, greenish yellow blacks they call "pistachios," and enough other quality pearls to concern the Tahitians. With the popularity of black pearls and their earning potential, farms are springing up all over the Pacific.

CULTURED FRESHWATER PEARLS

P earl lovers are indeed fortunate. Crystal gemstones usually originate in only a few sources, whereas any shelled mollusk in either fresh or saltwater is capable of producing pearls. The producers that come instantly to mind are mussels, oysters, clams, conch, and abalone. We usually bite down on the lovely small saltwater mussel pearls too late—after cooking has destroyed them as jewels. Pearls from freshwater mussels, which provide us with an historical link to early pearl gatherers, are, on the other hand, at the center of the liveliest activity in pearling today.

A great irony of pearl history is that the least expensive cultured pearl product in the market today rivals the quality of the most expensive natural pearls ever found. This price-value anomaly is obvious to consumers as they hasten to buy Chinese freshwater bargains. Only two other pearl types are solid nacre—natural saltwaters and natural freshwaters.

Natural freshwater pearls from mussels and natural saltwater pearls from oysters are very similar chemically and structurally. Natural freshwater pearls occur in mussels for the same reasons that saltwater pearls occur in oysters. Foreign material, usually a sharp object or parasite, enters a mussel and cannot be expelled. To reduce irritation, the mollusk coats the intruder with nacre, the same secretion it uses for shell building.

Most cultured freshwater pearls are composed entirely of nacre, just like their natural freshwater and natural saltwater counterparts. In contrast, the majority of a cultured saltwater pearl's volume is an implanted shell bead nucleus (pages 30-31), only coated with nacre, or mother-of-pearl, which can wear thin. Therefore, these solid nacre freshwater pearls are completely

Pearls of great color, round with high lustre, illustrate how far Chinese freshwater production has evolved since the 1970s. Investigation shows they are usually nucleated with shell beads or small pearls.

U.S. Pearl Company

John Latendresse operates pearl farms in Tennessee and Texas. In addition to his mother-of-pearl shapes and mabés, which he calls "domés," only John and the Chinese are producing shell- and pearl-nucleated round freshwater pearls.

unaffected by the short-culturing controversy that surrounds saltwater pearls. Culturing time affects tissue-cultured freshwater pearls only by determining how large they will grow.

The Chinese were the first to culture a product from freshwater mussels. Their "pearl Buddhas," made from the 1200s until this century, were not true pearls but shell mabés. The first cultured freshwater pearls originated in Japan. Quite soon after their initial success with cultured saltwater pearls, Japanese pearl farmers experimented with freshwater mussels in Lake Biwa, a large lake near Kyoto. Initial commercial freshwater pearl crops appeared in the 1930s. The all-nacre Biwa pearls formed in colors unseen in saltwater pearls. Almost instantly appealing, their lustre and luminescent depth rivaled naturals because they too were pearls throughout.

Even though World War II interrupted the flow of Lake Biwa pearls, by the 1950s strands sold in Japan as less expensive colorful alternatives to the mainstay material, cultured saltwater pearls. Biwas' success and publicity were so effective that until a few years ago, all freshwater pearls were routinely referred to as "Biwas," no matter their origin or that such references are illegal in the U.S. unless the pearls are actually from Biwa.

When I first visited Lake Biwa in 1973, freshwater pearl production still thrived. But, although the lake supplied most of the world's freshwater pearls, there were warning signs as development pressed toward its shores. On a return trip in 1984, I observed that Biwa's pearl farms were barely surviving. A burgeoning resort community on the lake's southern edge used septic tanks, which polluted the water with nutrients. The agricultural farmers who virtually surrounded the lake were applying herbicides and

Unlike new Chinese round pearls, most freshwater cultured pearls are still nucleated with pieces of mantle tissue (above) placed directly into a mussel's mantle to initiate nacre production. Up to 30 pearls can grow simultaneously in large animals (left). The original Lake Biwa pearls were superb (lower left), but pollution diminished the crop's quality (lower right).

pesticides, which of course washed into the water. Small factories had popped up near the lake's edge, adding their effluent, and a more affluent Japanese population had ringed Biwa with vacation homes, all bringing more untreated sewage and other pollution. Pearl crops had deteriorated along with water quality. Biwa was biologically near death, and the pearls showed it.

As so often happens in history, one industry declines while another rises. So it was with cultured freshwater pearls. As Biwa production diminished, China filled the vacuum. China has all the resources that Japan lacks: a huge land mass; countless available lakes, rivers, and irrigation ditches; a limitless and pliable work force that earns less than a dollar a day; and an almost desperate need for hard currency. In 1968, with no recent history in pearling, China startled the gem world with prodigious amounts of ridiculously inexpensive pearls. Unfortunately for China's reputation as a producer and for the impression left with the public, the initial Chinese offering, what

I call the First Chinese Pearl Wave, in the 1970s and 1980s, appeared trivial. Immediately dubbed "Rice Krispies," the oddly-shaped kernels with crinkly surfaces dyed any number of "pop" colors could in no way compete with the best from Lake Biwa. The Second Wave barely rippled the market but was an important evolutionary step. Between 1984 and 1991, China learned fast and well, mastering techniques and producing better shapes and colors (see opposite). Buying expertise from Japan and the U.S., the Chinese continued experimenting.

Now China is in what I call its Third Pearl Wave. Starting in the 1990s, China surprised the market with products that are revolutionizing pearling. As testimony to China's achievement, their freshwater pearls are round enough and good enough to pass as Japanese akoya. China already sells round white pearls up to 9.5mm for perhaps a fraction the price of Japanese cultured saltwater pearls.

B y now you are probably wondering how freshwater pearls can be cultured without nuclei. Once you have seen how cultured pearls are made, it is important to discern what Mikimoto's two predecessors discovered and what they invented. The shell bead nucleus inserted into the body of a saltwater oyster does not, by itself, start the production of nacre. To trigger the pearl-making process, technicians must implant a small live piece of mantle tissue alongside the nucleus. It is the mantle tissue that induces the oyster to produce a protective pearl sack, then coat the nucleus with nacre.

Unlike an oyster's mantle tissue, the mantle in a freshwater mussel is large and thick, covering the interior of both shells (see page 41). It is within this mantle tissue, not the body of the mussel, that cultured freshwater pearls

Chinese pearl production looks somewhat the same whether done in government lakes (above) or by citizens in neighborhood irrigation ditches (opposite). Second-generation pearls (left) were almost as good as the last from Lake Biwa before that production closed. Even under primitive conditions, the Chinese have revolutionized freshwater pearls.

form. At Lake Biwa the Japanese discovered it is possible but unnecessary to insert shell nuclei in order to get acceptable freshwater pearls. To culture freshwater mussels, workers slightly open their shells, cut small slits into the mantle tissue inside both shells (see page 41), and insert small pieces of live mantle tissue from another mussel into those slits. In freshwater mussels that insertion tissue alone is sufficient to start nacre production.

The Chinese learned almost by trial and error decades later that the placement and the shape of the inserted tissue is vital to the shape and quality of the finished pearl. The Japanese had shown at Lake Biwa that they could create bars, crosses, discs, and a variety of other shapes by altering the shapes of mantle tissue pieces. The Chinese realized the world wanted round pearls, so its nucleators concentrated on techniques to increase the percentage of rounds.

Those pearl developments inside China coincided with a loosening of economic constraints and movement toward enclaves of free-market capitalism. In the 1980s mussels were nucleated at government facilities and either grown on government farms or distributed to local rice farmers to tend in their irrigation ditches. There is even less central control over supply or price. Hong Kong and other merchants buy directly from farmers, bypassing the state system. I estimate that production is already more than 750 tons of Chinese freshwater pearls annually. Now that world demand for Chinese pearls is great and government controls over growers weak, thousands of pearl farms operate somewhat independently, which currently means there are great bargains. It also means erratic supplies and a lack of any quality control. My advice in such situations is that, if you see pearls you like at a fair

First stop after harvest in China is a warm, mild bleach bath under bright light, which transforms off-color and mottled pearls to white.

price, buy now because they may not be back again.

Although there is very little said about processing freshwater pearls, you should know that bleaching, dyeing, and polishing do occur. Except for the old Arabic practice of sun bleaching in the Persian Gulf, naturals were practically never processed. Chinese pearls that are nearly white or mottled are usually bleached in peroxide to make them whiter and more uniform. With the same methods perfected by the Japanese, the Chinese use a mild bleach, bright fluorescent lights, and heat (see above). They polish surfaces by tumbling pearls in pumice or similar substances. The idea, as always, is to facilitate matching pearls for strands. Many Chinese pearls used to be dyed in the 1980s to bright red, blue, lavender, yellow, or even black. In response to contemporary preferences, they now offer a selection of subtle natural colors.

China initially processed its own pearls. Today, with only a small domestic supply of freshwater pearls, Japan has been using its expertise to bleach and polish China's. As a result, Chinese freshwater pearls often arrive in the U.S. marked "Product of Japan," the same ploy the Japanese use in relabeling Chinese saltwater pearls.

The freshwater pearl market is rapidly adapting to new realities. Japan can no longer produce volumes of freshwater pearls because of its costs and its pollution. To stay in the pearl business, it needs to have products to process and sell. To do that, Japanese firms had to enter into agreements with China or various Chinese farms or individuals. The Japanese presence is already evident throughout China. Because Hong Kong reverted to Chinese control in 1997, after a century as a British colony, its

Crinkled Chinese pearls could wholesale for less than $1 a strand in part because young women using bowstrings to drill holes earned less than $1 a day.

pearl companies busily sought agreements assuring access to Chinese products. Such a rich mix of dealing and intrigue makes for great drama. But there will be no market and no commerce without one basic reality: China has to continue producing great freshwater pearls.

Just as Colombia sets the world standard for emeralds, the original Biwa pearls established a standard for cultured freshwater pearls that both dealers and consumers believed would never be surpassed. China has recently shaken that belief. The shapes, luster, and colors of the new Chinese production often match original Biwa quality and sometime even surpass it. Certainly the new orange or peach-colored pearls are unique. Biwa mussels never produced those colors naturally.

Round pearls are nature's exceptions. After looking at the new large round pearls made over the past few years, I suspected the Chinese were using a new process. I wondered if traditional freshwater techniques could produce such beautiful results. Many factors combine to create the more normal off-round results. The only reason saltwater pearls can be grown round in large quantities is because they are composed mainly of round shell nuclei. When the oyster lays down a relatively thin nacre coating over a spherical bead, there is little chance for the shape to vary far from round.

If I wanted to make round freshwater pearls, how would I do it? Tradition does not supply an answer; the Japanese were never consistently able to make round freshwater pearls. I might try to make better balls of mantle tissue. Next, I would question whether to use pure mantle-tissue nucleation at all. What if, instead of tissue, I made beads from shells of the same mussel species I used for culturing? Would that fool an x-ray appraisal?

Examples of the new Chinese pearl culture revolution exhibit round shapes, high lustre, and vivid natural colors. These are often favorably compared with Biwas.

I saw a sole Japanese pearl farmer experimenting with that in 1984. Or what if I took a bold step? What if I used worthless, badly-colored off-round pearls, tumbled them until they were round, then reinserted them, and let the mussels coat them with nacre?

Just as I conjectured, we now know that the Chinese are indeed practicing each and every one of those techniques today. The Chinese are nucleating some of their freshwater mussels with shell-nuclei implants in both the creatures' bodies as well as in their mantles. Such practices, once perceived as "saltwater culturing techniques," are a new cultural revolution. How will buyers react who had been told that cultured freshwater pearls were all-nacre products? Will they buy Chinese pearls if the roundest examples are nacre-coated shell beads instead? How will such new products be positioned in the market? Will anyone, including gem testing labs, be able to tell the difference between tissue-nucleated and pearl-nucleated freshwater pearls?

Those are serious new considerations that no one had admitted existed until this book. Even more disquieting is the second innovation. I confirmed that the Chinese are nucleating mussels with their own tissue-cultured freshwater pearls, which result in all-nacre round or almost round pearls. Aiming for an even higher percentage of rounds, the Chinese are reshaping some reject freshwater pearls into spheres, then nucleating mussels with them. When combined, those two nucleation innovations are astounding developments. Once again the Chinese have radically altered freshwater culturing, making saltwater and freshwater techniques indistinguishable. Some of China's new pearls are all nacre, some have nacre-coated nuclei, all are unmarked. One U.S. experimenter used small off-round American natural pearls as nuclei. He sent the resulting much larger cultured freshwater pearls to a gem lab and received a report identifying them as "naturals." If

In the mid-1990s the Chinese started showing round pearls priced at $10 to $200 a strand. To be this round, pearls are nucleated with shell beads or other pearls.

pearl farmers can grow cultured pearls that fool labs into believing they are naturals, the market may be in for a wild ride. Japan recently hybridized Chinese and Japanese mussels to produce even larger pearls, from 9mm all the way to 15mm, which can be confused with their South Sea saltwater cousins.

America's freshwater pearl impresario, John Latendresse, continues making the U.S. a force in pearl culturing. His recent work parallels the Chinese experiments in freshwater mussel nucleation. John implants shell nuclei up to $5^{1}/_{2}$mm in mantles to produce $8^{1}/_{2}$mm to 9mm pearls and up to 8mm beads and other shapes into the bodies of mussels, where they are coated to become pearls as large as 12mm. Latendresse also makes pearls shaped like coins, crosses, sticks, domes, bars, and drops. Once he even made pearls in the shape of Texas. He believes such innovations are the future of pearl culturing.

From the customer's viewpoint, this is a wonderful time to buy pearls. Rejoice that there are more choices than ever. Fortunately, most freshwater pearls are attractive and reasonably priced. Chinese rounds are typically shell-bead or pearl-bead nucleated. Shapes such as those made by Latendresse are also shell-nucleated. Off-round pearls are still produced by tissue nucleation.

Chinese pearls come in a gorgeous array of undyed, natural colors— peach, pink, orange, mauve, heather, and white. In addition to China, the largest volume producer, freshwater pearls come from Japan and the U.S. in sizes from 3mm to 15mm and prices from $10 to $10,000 a strand. With such a wide range of prices, shapes, and colors, you may want a selection of pearls for different outfits. My suggestion about purchasing cultured freshwater pearls is direct and simple: Buy now. They are attractive and durable bargains.

MOTHER-OF-PEARL AND SHELL PRODUCTS

M abé "pearls," "pearl" buttons, "pearl" gun and knife handles, "blister pearls" and the thousands of mother-of-pearl inlay pieces that form the temple door (opposite) are really not pearls at all. They are mother-of-pearl, or shell products. Far more objects from oceans and rivers are called pearls than should be. We need to define "pearl" terms and decide what to do about "pearly," "pearl-like," and mother-of-pearl. Mother-of-pearl has a grand tradition all its own. Although the entire shell of a mollusk is actually nacre, it is only the inner surfaces that the mollusk keeps highly polished that we call mother-of-pearl. Other shell parts can be polished to become mother-of-pearl. A piece of natural shell or an object glued to the shell and then coated with nacre is still mother-of-pearl.

What, then, is a pearl? If the mollusk deposits nacre on an object encased in its flesh, the product, however shaped, is a pearl. A pearl can form naturally, or it can form when a mollusk coats an implanted nucleus.

"Blister pearls," traditionally known as pearls, require their own definition. They result *naturally* when a piece of debris sticks to the inside of a shell or a parasite bores through from the outside. Either way, the mollusk coats the irritant. For clarity, I propose that even if a natural object is a bump or a slight dome, it is still mother-of-pearl. If it is half a sphere or more, it should be called a "blister pearl." Only pearls that grow in the mantle or body deserve to be called simply "pearls."

Mabés are the principal commercial objects produced on shells. While an oyster is out of the water for nucleation, small plastic half-domes are glued to the surfaces inside its shell. Back in the ocean, the oyster coats both the nucleus and the plastic domes with nacre. After harvesting, workers cut

Mother-of-pearl inlays, as on this Buddhist temple door in Bangkok, are one of the oldest and most consistent uses of pearl shells. Color, iridescence, and quality of workmanship determine value.

49

Pearl oyster shells are more valuable than the meat, which is used for animal food and fertilizer. Many pearl shells yield colorful mother-of-pearl, used for a variety of jewelry and decorative products (left).

Outside Mikimoto's factory in Toba (below), where Japanese pearl culturing began, a worker separates harvested shells with commercial quality mother-of-pearl.

Before plastic, mother-of-pearl buttons from oysters, mussels, and abalone (right) were ubiquitous. From the 1890s to the 1920s the U.S. was the world center for shell buttons, cutting billions of them from America's freshwater mussels.

Empress Abalone Ltd.

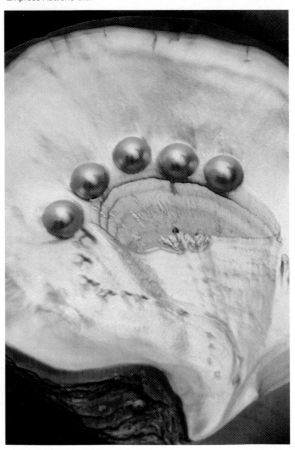

Mabés are really not pearls but mother-of-pearl domes made to order on the inside surfaces of shells. Although the Japanese take credit, the Chinese originated mabés and culturing in the 1200s. Some of the most colorful examples are abalone mabés (above) successfully cultured on New Zealand's Stewart Island.

Today's mabés are usually made in the South Seas. Plastic domes are glued onto shell surfaces. After the oyster coats the domes with nacre, the mabés (left) are core-drilled, separated from the plastic domes (below), filled with epoxy, then backed with mother-of-pearl.

Roebuck Deep Pearls (2)

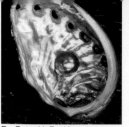
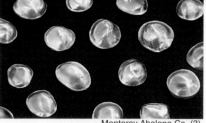

Dr. Peter V. Fankboner   Monterey Abalone Co. (3)

Abalone mabés are America's newest pearl products. Several companies along the California coast are attempting simultaneously to master keeping the creatures alive in tanks while creating a new market for their attractive domes. Baby abalones from state hatcheries provide the raw material (bottom, left). After nucleation, abalones live underwater on plastic sheets inside barrels (right) and coat their acrylic inserts (top left). After 2 to 3 years, the abalones produce saleable mother-of-pearl mabés (above, center).

mother-of-pearl domes from the shell, fill them with epoxy, back with another piece of mother-of-pearl, and sell them as mabé "pearls." Actually, they are not pearls at all, but mother-of-pearl domes.

Because mother-of-pearl is abundant and universally appealing, its use probably predates the use of pearls. To wear pearls and mother-of-pearl, primitives had to know how to drill them. But they could just break off a pretty piece of mother-of-pearl and carry it around. Attractive shells once were currency in many parts of the world.

For centuries most mother-of-pearl was used to make buttons. Originally buyers preferred the iridescence, or "orient," of Persian Gulf shells. Then the business shifted to U.S. freshwater mussels, the main source of mother-of-pearl buttons after 1891. Australia's shells gained favor about the same time, due mainly to their larger sizes. Today, mother-of-pearl buttons are visible markers of expensive and high-quality clothes.

Inlays and decorations for objects and jewelry have always been popular, especially now with more colorful specimens available, particularly abalone. In cottage industries, natives of Korea, China, Burma, Thailand, and Hong Kong hand craft boxes, necklaces, bracelets, serving knives, forks, and spoons in mother-of-pearl, usually cut from Australian and Tahitian shells.

Less well-known shell products sell mainly in Asia. China makes toothpaste, face cream, and calcium tablets. In Japan you can pop tablets of ground pearl as medical supplements. Because pearls and shells are calcium carbonate, such pills are probably helpful. Mr. Mikimoto swallowed one or two pearls a day all his long life. But, unless crushed, pearls are indigestible. In Japan, after all the other uses in beauty and health products, the remaining shells are ground up for fertilizer, the ultimate recycling.

53

IMITATION

PEARLS

Whether they are called "faux," "fake," "costume," "phony," or just plain "imitation," they are, to the trade, the same thing. They are beads in a wide variety of materials made to look like pearls. But there is nothing whatsoever in them that rightly allows them to be called pearls. They are not naturals, they are not cultured, they are not pearls.

Are they bad? No. Are they bargains? Some are. Can you get a great look, even a South Sea look, for a few dollars or a few hundred dollars? Yes.

Imitations used to be more of an affordable alternative than they are now that Chinese cultured freshwater pearls are so inexpensive. But the appeal of imitations is altogether different. They are made to look like expensive Japanese akoya cultured saltwater pearls, usually about 8mm. Some are made to look like South Sea pearls 10mm and larger. They come in the same variety of lengths as cultured pearls. These products may not fool the viewer, but they nevertheless make a fashion statement for a modest outlay.

Imitation pearls are not new. In fact, before this century of cultured pearls, the only way to own pearls was either to be very, very rich or to buy imitations. Now most working women can afford cultured pearls of some type or quality. Still, there is a vast market for imitations, worth tens of millions of dollars annually. Some young working buyers, who could perhaps afford a strand of small akoyas, prefer the versatility of owning several different lengths, colors, and sizes of imitations.

Although virtually every conceivable material has been used to imitate pearls, plastic is now the substance of choice. Cheap and easy to fabricate, it can be made in any color. Available solid or hollow, it can be coated or painted. Plastic beads are easy to detect with a bright penlight. When backlit, the plastic, which is uniform inside, glows evenly. You can tell if it is hollow or solid by its weight and by looking down a drill hole. The area around the drill hole also reveals whether the bead is simply painted, coated, or colored plastic. For those who like the flair of costume jewelry, these

If it looks like a pearl, wears like a pearl, but was not formed by an oyster or mussel, it is an imitation. Every strand to the left is just that. All these are varieties of plastic except the center bracelet, which is a Majorica, made by dipping glass beads into a mixture of fish scales.

Of all imitations, the least expensive to make are either all-plastic beads or plastic beads coated with paint, acrylic, or almost anything else that gives the impression of pearls. When backlit, such imitations appear uniformly clear, because they are uniform inside. Some plastic pearls are solid for additional weight, and some are hollow. No matter how they are made, plastic imitations are inexpensive look-alikes sold to produce a pearl appearance without a pearl price.

Majorica is the only brand name for imitations that the public recognizes. Made for over a century, first on the island Majorca in the Mediterranean and now in Spain, Majoricas begin as solid glass balls. Those are dipped up to seven times in a paste (which the company likes to call "pearl essence") of ground fish scales and adhesive. When backlit, Majoricas show a different texture from the far less expensive imitation plastic pearls.

To the inexperienced observer, a Majorica imitation pearl might appear to have a pearly iridescence (caused by the fish scales) and a surface texture that could even pass the "tooth test." But simple magnification reveals the truth. Around a drill hole the fish scale layers pull away from the glass bead inside and look nothing like cultured pearl nacre on a shell bead. The glass bead, seen here with the drill hole through it, is uniform, whereas a cultured pearl shell nucleus is textured. Majoricas are easy to detect.

imitations require very little care or concern. Solid dyed beads should last longer than painted or coated imitations. Usually it is the weak string, which is neither knotted nor silk, or the cheap clasp, which is not precious metal, that determines the life of the strand.

It is possible to buy better quality imitation pearls. If you want an 8mm akoya look, knotted beads, and a gold clasp, be prepared to pay $100 or more. The beads are no more valuable, but the necklace looks finished. Some stores and distributors specialize in and advertise this type product. Also, South Seas sizes, 10 to 20mm, are available in imitation pearls, but for considerably more.

Some imitations are made with acrylic or glass beads. Glass is heavier, which is usually a tip-off, and breakable. So be careful not to drop or subject it to hard knocks.

Another imitation actually uses shell bead nuclei like those inserted in oysters to produce cultured pearls. The shell nuclei for imitations are also coated, but not with nacre. Instead they are painted or dipped in paint, lacquer, or other materials to make them look like cultured pearls. This product has the right weight, even passing the x-ray and backlit tests. It does not pass the tooth test, because its surface is uniform instead of gritty. Magnification usually reveals the true character of the coating.

One imitation requires special mention, as it is the only brand in the group that has public recognition. "Majorica," a name kept before buyers through massive advertising, regularly appears in airline magazines, duty-free shops, and frequent promotions in upscale publications (see opposite). Little in the company's advertising reveals that Majoricas are imitations. Now made in Spain instead of on Majorca, the island in the Mediterranean, Majoricas are glass beads dipped into a fish scale and adhesive paste. The North Atlantic fish scales used are chosen for their iridescence. The process is clever, and the imitation itself has even been copied by other makers. The company says it applies up to seven coats of paste.

Majorica takes great care positioning itself as something else, at an in-between market position, priced way above other imitations and well below Japanese akoyas. I see Majorica necklaces advertised in catalogs and stores for $200 to $400. To its credit, the company does a good job of color matching and, with glass spheres at the core, supplies beads that are almost round. The problem I and others in the trade have with Majoricas is the confusion their advertising causes. I occasionally ask audiences for my pearl talk what they think Majoricas are. Most respondents mistakenly believe they are real pearls found or grown somewhere in the Mediterranean.

Generally with pearls, as with almost everything else in life, you really do get what you pay for. If you want imitation pearls, then by all means buy imitations. Remember that gold clasps and knotting should and do add more to the price. Make sure you buy a fairly uniform product, moderately well-made, that sells at the price of an imitation.

BUYING AND CARING

Gem and jewelry customers first want to know two things: What should I buy, and how should I take care of it? With pearls, smart buyers need to make additional decisions. Having read this far, you already know more than most other pearl customers. Now you can use what you know to buy well and protect your investment.

Cultured pearls account for almost all pearl sales today. Very few people buy natural pearls, which are now costly collectibles usually found at auctions. Japanese akoya hold an ever decreasing market share. Chinese freshwater pearls dominate volume sales while Chinese akoya gain against the Japanese every month. White and black South Sea pearls are enjoying enormous sales increases at the top of the market. With so many changes and so many new pearl products, the most important thing you need to know is how to determine quality and value in the pearls you want to buy.

Because the vast majority of pearls come in 16-inch necklace strands, that will be our discussion standard. Such strands with knots and a clasp finish to approximately 18 inches. Akoya necklaces of 5mm to 8mm retail for $500 to $5000 depending on quality and country of origin. Similar necklaces of 24 inches should cost a third more. Make significant purchases carefully, with sufficient information to assure you a fair product for a fair price.

When buying today's akoya, first consider nacre thickness; other factors are meaningless with nacre 0.3mm or less. I strongly recommend that you do not buy thinly coated pearls for any price or any reason. Only properly coated pearls will last an owner's lifetime and more. Insist that the seller measure and note on your sales receipt the nacre thickness of your new pearls. If for any reason the retailer is unable to do that, hire an appraiser who will, and have the results noted on your appraisal report. Ideally, nacre should be at least 0.4mm, which is measured either by x-ray or drill hole examination.

This elegant black and white South Sea cultured pearl necklace with diamonds set in gold perfectly illustrates a major point in gem care. Always clean jewelry with a procedure and with chemicals safe for the softest and most vulnerable component. In this case, the pearls and gold are equally soft, but pearls cannot withstand any acid or harsh chemical.
Necklace by Van Cleef & Arpels

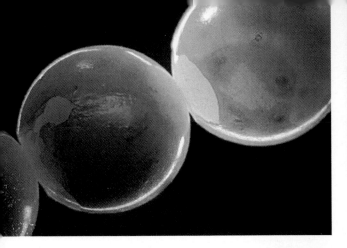

The only definitive method of separating naturals from cultured pearls is x-ray (above right), which in these cultured pearls clearly shows shell nuclei surrounded by nacre. Worthless short-cultured pearls, common from both Japan and China, have nacre so thin that it flakes off the bead (above). Almost transparent nacre caps from Indonesia fitted over blue or pink plastic domes create deceptively colored mabés (right).

Thickness of 0.4mm is the result of about a year and a half in the water. With the Japanese steadily cutting culturing time to half a year, you will see more 0.1mm and 0.2mm nacre than 0.4mm. My suggestion is to seek 0.4mm or more, which is now rare and expensive, but accept nothing less than 0.3mm, as represented by a jeweler or an appraiser.

When lustre is enhanced with polymer-coatings, a new enhancement technique, value comparisons are distorted. Study the chart on page 63 and its explanation on page 62. They clarify the relationships among lustre, blemishes, shape, color, and size. Remember that pearls are sold in every conceivable combination of those criteria. If you select a necklace combining the best examples of all five, it will cost the most. If you accept less than the best in any category, prices should drop. Be aware that with necklaces there is also a premium charged for good to perfect matches in roundness, size, lustre, blemishes, and color. Even with cultured pearls, it is difficult, time-consuming, and costly to deliver perfectly matched necklaces. But at top prices, you should expect such attention to detail.

Regular care is more important with pearls than with most other gems and jewelry you own. Pearls, soft delicate products from living creatures, are easily damaged by almost everything they contact. Following simple guidelines will allow you to enjoy your pearls for decades.

At Mohs 2½ to 4½, about the hardness of fingernails, pearls are softer

Pearls are delicate. Handle them carefully and avoid all acids and chemicals. Some skin oils are acidic, which damage pearls.

After being swallowed by a dog, the earring (above, left) dissolved in digestive fluids and reappeared a third its original size. Always apply perfume, hair spray, and other cosmetics before putting on pearls. Wipe each bead with a soft cloth after every use, and store necklaces in their own cloth bags.

than other gems, as well as virtually everything else you touch during the day. Store your pearls in cloth bags away from other jewelry. Be careful of hitting them against walls, countertops, tools, and all other hard objects that might crack or scratch them. Do not subject pearls to ultrasonic cleaners, steamers, detergents, cleaning solutions, or high heat. For additional information, refer to the pearls section of my new *Gem Care* book.

Not only are pearls soft but they are also alkaline, which means they are attacked by acids. Keep them from contacting hair spray, perfume, alcohol, cosmetics, bleach, ammonia, swimming pool water, and even acidic perspiration. This means you should apply perfume, cosmetics, and spray first, then put on your pearls, preferably atop clothes and not directly onto skin that may have chemical residues.

Restring pearls regularly, every two years with normal wear and annually with heavy use. Knot pearls to keep them from scattering if a string breaks and to reduce abrasion caused by grit in the atmosphere bound with skin oils on the strings. After every use, wipe your pearls with a soft cloth, damp or dry. If you feel you must wash pearls, use a soft, real, non-detergent soap, and do not rub individual pearls together. Rinse the strand with nothing hotter than warm water, pat with a clean cloth, then spread them on a soft towel to dry. Regular care will greatly extend the life of all your pearls, mabés, mother-of-pearl, conch cameos, and abalone.

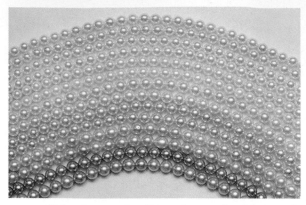

Color is a major factor in pearl pricing and appeal. Different countries like different colors, pink being the U.S. favorite. Japanese cultured pearls usually come in the above colors. Lustre is a gauge of surface polish. The pearls above right range from high lustre on top to flat.

Determining Pearl Quality...

Diamonds have their four "C's"; pearls have five criteria for determining quality, price, and value. The chart at right, originally prepared by *Modern Jeweler* Magazine and the Cultured Pearl Associations of America and Japan, graphically illustrates variations in lustre, surface, shape, color, and size. Although personal preferences affect your buying decision, it is also useful to know how the market responds to the five quality considerations.

Lustre and surface smoothness are equally important criteria. High lustre pearls with their mirror finishes are more desirable than flat or low lustre pearls. Also, everyone wants pearl surfaces as clean and smooth as possible. However, you do need to realize that low lustre, blemished pearls are sold. You should pay considerably less for them.

Shape is not a matter of quality, but taste. Unquestionably the most popular pearl shape for necklaces today is round. But that preference is a new phenomenon, unique to this century of cultured pearls. Many people enjoy ovals or choose drop shapes for earrings. Buyers who seek the unusual respond to the character of baroques, which often sell for a fraction of the cost of rounds.

Color is also a personal decision. A range of hues complements all colors of skin, hair, and eyes. Most Americans buy pink pearls. Europeans prefer cream or white. Middle Easterners like cream and gold, as do South Americans. Buy pearl colors the way you coordinate clothing. Choose what looks good on you.

Size dramatically affects prices, particularly over 7mm. People usually buy the largest pearls they can afford. Because pearl necklaces can be extended, you should first determine the size, color, and quality you want, then add length later. Adult women look best in 7mm to 10mm pearls.

With the information you have gathered in this book, you can buy beautiful, quality pearls that will give you years of enjoyment.